When the last British main line steam train ran on 11th August 1968, it was a finale in every sense. For the hundreds of thousands who had chased, ridden or just watched the antics of the last runs, it marked the

beginning of a drought. British Rail had declared that those engines that had been preserved were to be banished to private branch lines or museums. Apart from '*Flying Scotsman*' (for which a legal agreement pertained), there were to be no exceptions for we were entering a brave new world of modern trains. Nostalgia had no place in this scenario.

This seemed to be a challenge worth taking on and numerous attempts were made to breach the ban. By 1971 things changed and limited steam operations were allowed once more. Today the national network allows steam under controlled but increasingly difficult circumstances. We must savour it whilst we can!

Featured in this book are just some of the locomotives in the National Railway Collection that have returned to steam since they were preserved. There are plenty more and I apologise to those whose favourites have been omitted. I have tried to give the flavour of each featured locomotive and tell the story behind its inclusion. Unlike privately preserved locomotives, these are owned by the nation. It is incredible to see how many are **STEAMING ON...**

IAN R SMITH
YORK

12/7/05

Above: GWR 4-4-0 3440 'City of Truro' delights a group of readers of the magazine 'Steam Railway'. They had sponsored its overhaul and this was its public return to steam, at Cheltenham Racecourse, on the Gloucestershire Warwickshire Railway, on 2nd April 2004.

Front Cover: 4472 Now part of the National Railway Collection following 41 years in private preservation, 'Flying Scotsman' is arguably the most famous locomotive in the world. It is seen at York on 30th July 2003, in LNER livery but with German-style smoke deflectors and double chimney, as carried in its last couple of years in service with British Railways.

Imagine what a Grand Prix might have been like in 1829. One such event occurred at Rainhill, ten miles east of Liverpool. The directors of the new Liverpool and Manchester Railway had taken the decision that their railway would not have horses pulling the trains, and that they would carry both passengers and goods. In order to get the best locomotive design they had decided to hold a sort of Grand Prix. The prize for the best locomotive was £500 plus the contract to supply more to operate the line then under construction. The Trials would last for a couple of weeks and would be open to the public.

It was 6th October, a fine autumn Tuesday, and the crowds were there to enjoy themselves. All the roads in the area were choked with traffic as horse-drawn carriages made their way through the throngs of people on foot. A band played the popular music of the day and the sense of excitement increased as the directors of the railway, each wearing a white lapel ribbon, took their places to watch the proceedings at around ten o'clock.

By the time that the Trials began the crowds were packed like sardines for a mile and a half on

Above: The impressive but defeated hero of Rainhill. The reproduction 'Sans Pareil' at the Museum of Science and Industry in Manchester, May 1980.

Left: The reproduction 'Rocket' and matching Liverpool and Manchester Railway coach at the National Railway Museum, York, 27th September 1985.

both sides of the track. Not being used to seeing a train they did not realise that they should stand back. The two hundred special constables had a difficult time in crowd control.

First off was Stephenson's engine 'Rocket'. Built by Robert Stephenson (son of George, the engineer building the line) at his factory in Newcastle-upon-Tyne, it had been shipped around the coast to Liverpool, as there was no way it could be transported such a distance across the country.

The crowds gasped with both alarm and exhilaration as 'Rocket' accelerated along the line. All those fears about cows not giving milk and hens not laying eggs must have come to mind as the yellow monster cavorted its way along the line making a 'chuffing' sound. With smoke coming out of the tall chimney and steam from the times its own weight. 'Novelty' was unable to compete effectively on subsequent days because of mechanical problems. Nevertheless it was clear favourite with the crowds who tended to think of 'Rocket' as big, ugly and dirty.

By the time the second week dawned, Stephenson had a serious rival. Timothy Hackworth had built 'Sans Pareil' at his workshops in Shildon, County Durham. Working alongside George Stephenson's earlier railway, the Stockton and Darlington, he knew the kind of work that an engine would face on the new line. It had to be rugged and strong. Speed was fine but it was lower in the list of priorities.

'Sans Pareil' was able to compete for a while but after two hours it broke down and had to be pushed back by the spectators. It never recovered and was finally ruled out on grounds of being too heavy.

All through that fortnight, 'Rocket' kept appearing, reaching higher speeds and pulling greater loads. It fulfilled the conditions and won. George Stephenson went on to complete the railway that became the first public railway - in one way the first Inter-City railway. Robert Stephenson learned the lessons of the Trials and picked up an order for four engines based on 'Rocket'. Developments in technology were advancing so fast that even a year later, at the opening of the line, 'Rocket' was both a star and considered old fashioned. The four engines that came from Stephenson were much faster, more powerful and more reliable than their forebear. Indeed 'Rocket' only survived with the Liverpool and

Contrast in size. Stephenson's 'Rocket' meets the broad gauge 'Iron Duke' at York, 27th September 1985.

cylinders, people were terrified. They pushed back from the trackside and some fell over in the rush to stand clear.

Next engine off the blocks was 'Novelty'. Now here was an engine to delight the crowds. Small, neat and beautifully presented in its green livery, it was every bit the speed bird. Whilst 'Rocket' had pulled its train at a steady ten miles an hour, and then eighteen miles per hour on its own, 'Novelty' rushed off at twenty-eight miles per hour when on its own.

Of course one of the criteria of the Trials was that each locomotive should pull three

Manchester for a few years before being pensioned off to work at a coalmine in Cumbria.

The original 'Rocket', much rebuilt, was finally given to the nation and is normally on view at the Science Museum in South Kensington, London. Working reproduction versions of 'Rocket', 'Sans Pareil' and 'Novelty' were built ready for the celebration of 150 years since the opening of the Liverpool and Manchester Railway. Held in May 1980 at Rainhill, all three locomotives were in steam but just as in 1829 there were technical problems. 'Rocket' derailed in the sidings, 'Sans Pareil' had to be towed by a diesel shunter, and 'Novelty' was elegantly displayed on a flat wagon!

In 2003 however, the three locomotives were reunited for a real test (on the Llangollen Railway, in North Wales). The outcome was surprising in that each locomotive did much better than their 1829 prototypes – but once again 'Rocket' was the clear winner!

The working 'Rocket' is usually at the National Railway Museum in York, although it has been to Japan, the USA and the Netherlands. Both the original and reproduction versions of 'Sans Pareil' can usually be seen at 'Locomotion, the National Railway Museum at Shildon' in County Durham. 'Novelty' resides at the railway museum in Gävle, Sweden.

The handsome lines of the broad gauge 'Iron Duke' tower over the miniature train hauled by 'Margaret' at the National Railway Museum, York, on 9th September 1990.

The first public railways were built to the same track gauge as that adopted by the Stephensons in the north of England. There are various suggestions about how that gauge (4 feet 8 ½ inches – 1435mm) came about but there is no doubt that it was important that some form of standardisation should be agreed if trains were to run from one line to another.

In contrast, the new Great Western Railway from London to Bristol was designed by Isambard Kingdom Brunel to be a high-speed route, aligned with few sharp curves and gentle gradients. The purpose was to get people and goods from end to end as quickly as possible.

Brunel looked with disdain at the constricted lines built to Stephenson's gauge as they spread from the north towards London. He built his line to a huge track gauge of 7 feet and ½ inch (2150 mm). This allowed trains to go faster, more smoothly. Daniel Gooch was in charge of locomotive design. His 'Iron Duke' of 1847 was built to huge proportions. It sat between its frames and rode very smoothly.

Whilst technical excellence was something to be sought it is worth looking at the conditions for the driver and fireman. They were expected to stand on the footplate, exposed to the weather. Imagine driving west to Bristol in the teeth of a winter's storm. Even in summer, there was nowhere to sit down.

Conditions for passengers were also fairly spartan. The third class carriages were open to the elements, had no springs, rode like goods wagons, and had no seats. After official complaints were made, the Great Western reluctantly put a roof over third class heads, but did not provide windows.

The broad gauge was an incredible concept but the Great Western, and its dependent companies, was alone in choosing it. Everywhere else Stephenson's gauge spread rapidly. It was cheaper and it could enable connections to be made between adjoining railways. Eventually even the GWR fell into line and the last conversion to 'Standard' gauge took place in 1892.

The National Railway Museum locomotive 'Iron Duke' is a reproduction, built in 1985, as part of the celebration of the 150th Anniversary of the setting up of the GWR.

When engine 790 'Hardwicke' took over the night express from London Euston to Aberdeen at Crewe on the night of 22/23 August 1895, it was clear that something was afoot. Throughout that summer the night trains running north from both Kings Cross and Euston had raced one another to reach Aberdeen, often with little consideration for the comfort or convenience of their passengers. This was all about publicity. The newspapers were on the case and reported back on every new development to a readership that revelled in the way distant cities were being made to seem less far apart.

The hot August night afforded little comfort for those on board. Carriage windows had to be open. The noise and coal smuts from the engine had hammered their presence on to everyone on board. The wooden coaches held little in the way of comfort for those passengers travelling third class. They would have felt every rail joint and set of points as they had hurtled their way north from London in 148 minutes – a record that would stand for another four decades.

Standing on the platform at Crewe that night those travellers who were determined to stretch their legs would have noticed the coal piled high on the tender, and the steam roaring out of the impatient safety valves. They might have wondered about the capability of the diminutive engine now being attached. But they need not have had such thoughts. The night was to be one in which the records would fall.

After only a few minutes from arrival, 'Hardwicke' was off like a greyhound from the stocks. Word had gone out that no delays to this train were admissible. Ahead lay the racing stretch through Lancaster and Carnforth but, more significantly, the huge climb from sea level to Shap summit (915 ft). The first part of the climb, through Oxenholme, was taken at great speed. The noise from the little engine was fearsome as it roared defiance at the incline. Then came the steeper climb of Shap Fell. The exhaust from the chimney was awesome as 'Hardwicke' was coaxed to even greater effort. By the time the summit was cleared, a 'flying' average of 66.5mph had been achieved over the 104.8 miles since Minshull Vernon (just north of Crewe). The average speed from Carnforth to Shap Summit (58 miles) was 62.4mph, a route on which the average gradient was 1 in 185.

You might have imagined that, after that prodigious effort, the crew on the locomotive might ease off for the downhill section to Penrith and Carlisle. Not a bit of it! They leaned forward and 'Hardwicke' roared off into the night touching speeds of around 90mph. The 24.5 miles from Shap Station to Wreay (near Carlisle) were covered in 18.75 minutes at an astonishing 78.5mph.

By the time 'Hardwicke' was uncoupled at Carlisle, and the Caledonian Railway locomotive took over, the West Coast route was in pole position. Aberdeen was reached in only 512 minutes at an average start to stop speed of 63.2 mph.

'Hardwicke' is a 2-4-0 of the London & North Western Railway 'Precedent' Class. Upon withdrawal it was stored for a number of years at Crewe Works and other places before becoming a key exhibit in the National Railway Museum in York.

The diminutive LNWR 790 'Hardwicke' was unusually paired with another record-breaker, LNER 4472 'Flying Scotsman' prior to hauling a special train from Hellifield to Carnforth on 1st May 1975. The pair are seen at Carnforth. (Eric Treacy/NRM).

London Waterloo today is a bright attractive station, with graceful steel and glass roofing. It was not always thus. In the nineteenth century it was an untidy place with platforms having grown up amongst offices, stairways and passages. It was a mirror of much of Victorian London. Dirt was everywhere, hygiene was a new art, and all those coal fires and steam engines caused pollution on a grand scale. It is not surprising that as prosperity increased, those who could afford it preferred to live in leafy Surrey, or further afield. At the time the suburban trains serving Waterloo were hauled by the likes of the Beattie Well Tank, built in 1875. The capacity to haul increasingly faster, heavier trains was strained and so they had been superseded by 1898.

However three were to avoid the cutter's torch in 1898. The Wenford Bridge to Bodmin branch in Cornwall was short, and had tight curves. The heavy china clay trains did not require speed but they needed traction that allowed more wagons on each train. Their light weight, short wheelbase, and strength, was ideal for this work, and they settled down in this far-flung outpost of the London and South Western Railway.

In 1962 the Southern Region lines in the south west of England were transferred into the Western Region. The new managers had no warm feelings towards these ancient locomotives and quickly arranged for lightweight pannier tanks from the Great Western tradition to take over.

Of course their age alone was sufficient to account for the great affection being felt for these Victorian survivors. However, this connection with a long-gone era, and the well tank arrangement ensured that one was claimed for the National Railway Collection. Another went to private preservation. The third was scrapped....its charmed life over.

The pannier tanks operated the line from Wenford Bridge to Bodmin for only a few years before diesel shunters took over. The line itself closed and the china clay traffic went over to road haulage in the late 1980s.

30587, the engine claimed for the National Railway Collection, was for many years given a secure home not too far from its Cornish base, at Buckfastleigh on the Dart Valley Railway. It formed an attractive centrepiece in the museum. In an imaginative arrangement 30587 has been

Beattie Well Tank 30857 pulls a demonstration goods train including a Cornish clay 'hood' from its days on the Wenford Bridge branch. York 28th July 2003.

By the time that the Well Tanks were replaced they were nearly 25 years old. They had been run into the ground trying to keep pace with ever-increasing demands and it was almost inevitable that they would be sent for scrap. Their inability to go far without taking fresh supplies of water and coal restricted most alternative uses.

restored to running order and spends the summer months in steam at the National Railway Museum in York, whilst the rest of the year it is under the care of the Bodmin Steam Railway (who also allow it to visit other railway venues from time to time).

Beattie was the locomotive superintendent of the London & South Western Railway under whose direction these locomotives were built. The term 'Well Tank' refers to an arrangement whereby the water was contained in a tank underneath the boiler. It was a comparatively unusual arrangement in Britain and was not usually favoured, as it did not allow the locomotive to go very far without replenishing its water reserves.

Charles Rous-Martin had travelled overnight to Plymouth from London. Excitement mounted as he made his way from North Road to the Great Western Railway's Millbay Station. He had a good reputation as an impartial timer of trains and, at fairly short notice, had been invited by the GWR to travel on the mail train that would meet the liner coming in from New York on 9th May 1904. There was an inference that some kind of speed record might be attempted.

His train to Plymouth had been on time but the German steamer, 'Kronprinz Wilhelm', had arrived earlier than he had anticipated and the mail train had already been loaded by the time Rous-Martin climbed on board. No time for breakfast then!

A small tank engine moved the mail train to the dock gates before handing over to the year-old 4-4-0 No 3440 'City of Truro'. Moses Clements, of Exeter, was driver. He knew his locomotive and was aware that special arrangements had been made to clear the route. There would be a fast run with no delays caused by other trains in front.

As 'City of Truro' whistled before setting off with its special mail train of five vans, Rous-Martin leaned against an open droplight window looking out for the all-important quarter mileposts. These would provide the information against which the speed would be calculated.

That morning all was well and the locomotive hammered its way over the hills of South Devon,

3440 'City of Truro' pauses at Winchcombe on the Gloucestershire Warwickshire Railway, with a train from Cheltenham Race Course to Toddington on 2nd April 2004.

rushed alongside the sea wall at Teignmouth, before slowing to thread the intricate points at Exeter St David's. Then came the long climb up the Culm Valley. By now the exhaust from the engine was thundering and Rous-Martin was aware that, if the train was going to climb the incline so fast, then its descent would be something of a record. And so it proved. The top of the incline is just before Whiteball Tunnel and, by the time the train came out the other side, it was rocketing. Some of the postal workers were by now at the windows, aware that something unusual was happening as the train accelerated faster…and faster. Maybe platelayers were spotted on the lineside, or perhaps Driver Moses felt that enough was enough. Whatever the reason, the brakes were applied around Wellington and speed was brought down to more usual levels by the time they passed through Taunton.

At the end of the run, Rous-Martin maintained that after Whiteball the train broke the elusive 100 miles per hour barrier, touching a record 102.3 miles per hour. But how accurate was this? Certainly there is evidence to suggest that the locomotive in its original condition would have been capable of such a feat. However the ability of Rous-Martin (or anyone), standing by an open window, to log such speeds with the precision required is the main centre of controversy.

The reliance on a hand-held mechanical stopwatch linked to the observation and recording of quarter-mile posts was bound to result in some significant error at such speeds. Nevertheless, whatever the speed attained, it was undoubtedly the fastest any steam train had been able to travel whilst in commercial use.

It was this event that ensured preservation for 'City of Truro'. As a result of generous donations by readers of 'Steam Railway' and collaboration with a variety of preservation groups, it is remarkable that the centenarian should still be giving opportunities for the public to travel behind it – albeit at lower speeds than it was doing on 9th May 1904.

In the later years of the Nineteenth Century some amazing locomotives were produced. Not only did they have to be on the cutting edge of technological excellence, but also railway company directors wanted their locomotives to look graceful.

When the two main routes from London to Scotland (from Euston and King's Cross) were involved in what effectively became races, the Great Northern Railway (London to York) provided a most elegant locomotive. Patrick Stirling's 'Single' of 1870 might look fragile compared to the big engines that came in the next century, but it could pack a punch. Built with huge (eight foot) single driving wheels, once speed had built up this was a real flyer.

Whilst a 'Single' was able to turn in a good speed it was prone to difficulties in starting. It was important not to overload them as this could cause a 'Single' to slip. Thus trains on this route were usually lightweight.

By the beginning of the Twentieth Century, the new carriages were heavier and numbers of people travelling were increasing so the Stirling 'Single' was relegated to less arduous duties. The writing was on the wall. An ageing locomotive designed for lightweight high-speed runs was not particularly useful on stopping trains. No1, the first one produced, was withdrawn from service in 1907 but was kept as a museum piece.

The problem of a successor to the 'Single' was found in a bigger locomotive. By having four coupled driving wheels it was possible to haul heavier trains whilst having less tendency to slip. More wheels meant that it was possible to use the greater length to support a larger fire grate and a longer boiler. In turn, this enabled more power to be supplied to the cylinders.

The first one was 990 'Henry Oakley' and, when it came out of Doncaster works in 1898, its designer HG Ivatt was rightly proud of it. The first British tender locomotive built to the 'Atlantic' wheel arrangement, it was an immediate success. The class eventually totalled 22, and they were known as 'Klondykes'. However their reign on front line express work was short-lived as bigger locomotives soon appeared. Unlike the 'Single', the 'Klondyke' was more adaptable and soon settled down to a second career of hauling semi-fast stopping trains across the Great Northern network.

'Henry Oakley' was withdrawn in 1935, having covered 1,250,000 miles. It was placed in the original York Railway Museum.

The reason why the 'Klondykes' were relegated to less arduous work was the appearance of their larger cousins only four years later. Ivatt introduced his large-boilered 'Atlantic' in 1902 and very quickly it was taking over all the prestigious and heavy trains between King's Cross and York. For the next quarter century they held sway, until finally displaced by Gresley's Pacifics from the mid-1920s. Even then they could still be called on to deputise with great credit.

251 is one of a total of 94 that were eventually constructed. It was withdrawn by the LNER in 1947 for display at York. However in 1953 it was restored to working order and played an important role in the centenary celebrations at Doncaster works, along with its smaller cousin, 'Henry Oakley'.

990 'Henry Oakley' is to be seen at the Bressingham Steam Museum, Diss, Norfolk. The Stirling 'Single' is normally seen at the National Railway Museum in York, whilst 251 is on display at 'Locomotion, the National Railway Museum at Shildon'.

On 27th September 1953, both 990 'Henry Oakley' and 251 were brought out of museum status in order to work special trains from King's Cross to Doncaster. This was in connection with the centenary of the great railway works at Doncaster. Here the pair are seen at Great Ponton. (John Edgington).

Many of the railways of Britain are the result of the amalgamation of small companies serving towns in a particular area. The excitement of some of the high-speed railways in places like France and Japan is the result of building new lines, usually carving out a direct route between distant cities, and certainly not having the complication of lots of junctions. On such routes fast trains are unhindered by a variety of freight or local stopping trains. In 2003 the first such railway opened in Britain, as part of the Channel Tunnel to London line.

Way back in the nineteenth century the Channel Tunnel was a distant dream. Plans existed for a tunnel lit by gas and it was hoped that, one day, trains would run direct from the North of England to the Continent. Sir Edward Watkin was one such dreamer. By a series of moves he became chairman of a number of railways that, in alliance, might give direct access from the North to the English Channel. He was involved in the Tunnel project too. But there was a problem. From the East Midlands to London, trains in his alliance would have to be taken along the routes of his competitors.

There was only one answer. Build a new line. The resulting new route connected with the existing lines in the East Midlands and joined up with the Metropolitan in the Home Counties. The new line, along with the Manchester, Sheffield and Lincolnshire Railway was called the Great Central Railway (GCR). It was a magnificent line, built for high speed with fewer junctions than might be expected. Significantly the loading gauge (mainly the height of bridges) was built to European proportions so that trains one day might run direct from the continent.

The GCR London Extension opened in 1899. Its trains were stylish and its locomotives graceful. By the end of the first decade of the twentieth century trains on the GCR were significantly heavier than when the line opened. Robinson, the Chief Mechanical Engineer of the GCR, brought out a few large locomotives to meet the need. However it was the 'Director' Class, the first example being released in 1913, that was the real star. It was efficient and fast. Of all of Robinson's express locomotives, it is unlikely that anyone would have predicted that the 'Director' would have been such a success when it first came out.

Apart from their legendary performance on the GCR London Extension, after the formation of the London and North Eastern Railway in 1922, they were seen over other parts of the system. Indeed a version was cloned to operate in Scotland. They were particularly associated in their later years with the Cheshire Lines system from Manchester Central to Chester Northgate and Liverpool Central, as well as lines radiating from Sheffield Victoria. By 1960 the last few had gone, but not before 62660 *Butler Henderson* had been saved for preservation in the National Railway Collection.

In preservation, 'Butler Henderson' has appeared in both GCR and British Railways livery in steam and on display. As the only survivor of a long line of GCR passenger locomotives, it is very special. Normally it is on display at York.

The graceful lines and commodious cab of 506 'Butler Henderson' are shown to good effect in this view of the locomotive at Romiley in 1960, shortly after being restored at its birthplace Gorton Works. (BRB/NRM).

Preserved in British Railways livery as 63601, the only surviving 'Tiny' in Britain was restored following an appeal to the readers of 'Steam Railway'. Here the locomotive is seen at Leicester North on the Great Central Railway on 22nd March 2003.

was a long uphill section that reached its summit inside the great Woodhead Tunnel. As the line connected busy industrial areas there was an immediate need for goods trains. They slogged their way up to the suffocating confines of the Tunnel in both directions, like a conveyor belt, night and day.

Of course in the earliest days the goods trains were short and slow, but as time went on they became longer. Great trains of coal, or steel, or imported goods from Liverpool became the norm. Usually two engines on the front and at least one pushing on the back would rush at the long climb up to Woodhead. Imagine the conditions on the footplate as the engines thumped their way into the narrow single bore of Woodhead Tunnel. The crew would leave the engine on full regulator then crouch down in a corner with wet cloths over their mouths. The hot acrid smoke and steam from their own locomotive would squeeze its way into the cab and do a good attempt at asphyxiation on the crew. If they were on the second or banking locomotive the problem was multiplied.

Robinson, the Chief Mechanical Engineer of the Great Central Railway (GCR), was faced

Brooding over the Peak district between Sheffield and Manchester is a large granite mass surmounted by inhospitable peat bogs. Its highest point is known as Kinder Scout but the range of hills that shoulder it present a phalanx against travellers hoping to go between the two cities. Even today no motorway has succeeded in connecting the two cities directly.

One of the earliest railways in England was that which connected Sheffield with Manchester. It was a winner from the day it opened. But it was a difficult line to build and to operate. From both cities there

with a problem. Trains were getting longer and heavier but the small engines were not really up to the task. He played around with several ideas but the best response was a massive (for those times) locomotive with a 2-8-0 wheel arrangement. The first appeared in 1911 and the nickname of 'Tiny' soon followed. Compared with what had gone before they were gargantuan.

From the start they were a success, but after the outbreak of hostilities in 1914 (we call it the First World War) the design was adopted as standard by the Ministry of Munitions. This resulted in special construction of the class to serve overseas. In the final analysis, 666 locomotives of this type were built, placing them amongst the most numerous class ever built in Britain. After the war, hundreds returned and they were offered for sale to other railways. Some even went to Australia and China.

During the Second World War, the Government requisitioned 92 locomotives from the LNER list, taking them to the countries of the Eastern Mediterranean. They never returned, some lasting in Egypt until the 1960s.

Of those remaining in Britain, some survived until 1966. However it was the Australian locomotives that kept going longest, only being withdrawn from service in 1973.

In preservation 63601 is part of the National Railway Collection. It is normally kept at Loughborough, appropriately on the preserved section of the Great Central Railway. In Australia there are three examples preserved.

After the First World War all the railways needed more powerful goods engines. Because the wagons had no brakes the trains were not required to go fast, but it made economic sense for them to be longer. If one bigger engine rather than two smaller ones could do the work then that was going to be a bonus. On the London and North Western Railway (LNWR) the answer lay in the development of a series of engines with eight coupled driving wheels. Built to this pattern, but delivered to the company that took over the LNWR, the London Midland and Scottish (LMS), the G2 (nicknamed the 'Super D') 9395 came into traffic in 1921.

This type of locomotive was extraordinary in that it had a very basic layout, and certainly there was no concession to driver comfort, but was very strong and reliable. It would pull goods trains all over the former LNWR system but its supremacy would not last. By the mid-1930s it was superseded by Stanier's 8F, being more powerful, with more comfort in the cab. Nevertheless the 'Super D' was still used for lines where weight restrictions prevented the 8F from operating, and in those places there was nothing to match it until the diesels came in the 1960s.

Across the Lancashire Coalfield the 'Super D' was king. At places like Kenyon Junction on Stephenson's Liverpool to Manchester line there would often be a couple of these engines making up their trains prior to heading off over the bumpy route to Bolton. Imagine a foggy day, with gas lamps humming away in the station waiting room. Outside in the damp, sulphurous fog, the sound of the 'Super D' shunting was always marked by a distinctive wheeze that seemed to match the bronchial problems of many of the local people. Then the engine whistle would shriek and with a mighty clatter the coal wagons would follow the chesty sound of the locomotive. The struggle to get the train to move would cause a great deal of oscillation as the engine seemed to waddle sideways in its effort to command the reluctant weight of the train.

Gradually all the LNWR's locomotives were consigned to the scrap heap but a remnant of the 'Super D' Class outlived most of their compatriots by over a decade. Until forty years ago, a railway line used to thread a fairly precarious route across the bleak moorland above Buxton in Derbyshire. It went to the market town of Ashbourne. In the days when the railways carried a lot of goods this line was important but it was restricted in that the larger goods engines that were built after the mid-1930s were too heavy. As a result the 'Super D' found its niche on this line. It was both powerful and able to satisfy the weight restrictions that the more modern 8F or WD engines could not. But it was old and showing signs of its age.

Wheezing along the line one day 49395 was hauling the local goods train when

The rugged lines of the 'Super D' are seen in this view of 49395 at Bescot in the 1950s. The young railwayman is not known, and neither is the photographer. (NRM).

STEAMING ON

it suffered what in those days amounted to a terminal failure. Water managed to get into one of the cylinders and the resulting expansion cracked the metal. The remedy would be to provide a new cylinder or scrap the engine. For reasons of economy the latter course was chosen and the locomotive was towed to Uttoxeter shed, where it was dumped.

As a class, the 'Super D' had outlived most other standard gauge LNWR classes by over a decade. The British Transport Commission was looking to preserve an example. 49395, the first of the G2 Class to be built, was chosen. As the locomotive would be a static exhibit, a cracked cylinder was of no consequence and 49395 looked otherwise to be a good example to preserve. In practice it has been a difficult choice. In service it was a notorious locomotive, and the staff at its last home depot of Buxton would have preferred the excellent performing 49446 to have been saved.

Since then it has had a chequered history. Stored in various locations, sometimes out of doors and exposed to the worst of the elements, 49395 presented a sorry case when in 1993 it was announced that TV celebrity and pop music impresario Pete Waterman would partner the National Railway Museum in its restoration. By then technology had developed to the extent that the cracked cylinder was now repairable using a new process called stitch welding. But the path has been a slow one. Having taken over a decade to restore the locomotive its return to steam is one of the most remarkable features of recent preservation history.

CLIMBING TO CONSETT

In County Durham a massive steel works used to exist high on the Pennines at Consett. As its original supplies of raw materials had diminished it became increasingly necessary to bring in all the raw materials such as iron ore, coal and limestone. Latterly the iron ore was imported via Tyne Dock. This resulted in very heavy trains being used on a route that climbed a thousand feet in only a few miles. It required very special locomotives.

One type of engine associated with the line was the North Eastern Railway's T3 Class. Having eight coupled wheels, three cylinders, a massive boiler, and a capacious cab to protect the crew from the ravages of Pennine winters, the T3 was designed by Vincent Raven and introduced in 1919. For over 40 years this class of 15 locomotives would hammer its way up the severe gradients to Consett. Whilst more modern locomotives, such as the 9F, arrived in the mid-1950s, these engines were only consigned for scrap with the arrival of diesels.

Fortunately the first of the class, British Railways 63460 (NER No901) was saved for the National Railway Collection. It has been seen in preservation operating on the North Yorkshire Moors Railway but is now appropriately back in County Durham at 'Locomotion, the National Railway Museum at Shildon'.

The massive presence of the T3 class of the North Eastern Railway is clear in this view of 901 at Grosmont on the North Yorkshire Moors Railway on 16th September 1990.

'King Arthur' Class 777 'Sir Lamiel' gets into its stride, leaving York with the 'Scarborough Spa Express' on 9th July 1985.

Amongst the youthful people standing on Wimbledon station in 1962 there was great excitement every time an express raced through. For trains to Bournemouth or Weymouth, or to the West of England, the engine on the front was usually one of Bulleid's Pacifics. The howling whistle and the swaying train made people stand back and watch until the last coach raced out of sight, leaving only the lingering smell of smoke.

In contrast, who would turn to notice the shabby locomotive drifting by at the head of a line of varied goods wagons? It might have been one of the last of the once-revered *'King Arthur'* class. How were the mighty fallen. Increasing electrification of the railways in Kent had displaced the Pacifics and they, in turn, were replacing the *'King Arthur'* and *'Lord Nelson'* locomotives on the lines out of Waterloo. Both types of engine were classics in their own right, but now they were in the twilight years hauling semi-fast trains to Basingstoke or goods trains to Feltham.

The *'King Arthur'* class had been designed in the days after the First World War. The growing importance of the port of Southampton during the 1920s meant that trains serving the great liners had to be heavier and faster. Speed had always been a tradition on this route but it had meant that short trains or two locomotives on each train had become necessary. Something that would fit the demand for both speed and strength was met by the introduction of a new design of locomotive that was named after characters in the legends of King Arthur.

The *'Arthurs'* quickly found acceptance right across the Southern Railway network and they were also used to haul the holiday trains, originating in the North and Midlands. One of the most famous railway posters of all time was produced at this time. Showing a tiny child looking up to the driver of an *'Arthur'*, the boy declared, 'I'm taking an early holiday 'cos I know summer comes early in the south'.

One of the other criteria for locomotives on the Southern Railway was the ability to accelerate quickly in order that they could operate on routes that had been electrified. Steam trains normally start slowly and build up speed but that would play havoc with all the electric trains, as they start and stop quickly. That requirement, as well as the need to haul even heavier trains at consistently higher speeds, resulted in a real thoroughbred locomotive, the 'Lord Nelson' class.

The Southampton boat trains were particularly associated with the 'Nelsons'. Pulling 500 tons from the Ocean Terminal situated alongside the transatlantic liners they had to get into a rhythm of speed very quickly. By the time the train reached Eastleigh it would be bowling along. To those on the platform, the approach of the boat train would have a distinctive sound. A 'Nelson' on the train would sound like a well-tuned sewing machine, rather than the roar of, say, an 'Arthur'. This was the result of a special arrangement of the cranks that gave eight 'chuffs' to each wheel revolution compared to the more usual four. This was not just a whim, it gave better acceleration and was especially important in the London suburbs.

From the time they were built in the mid 1920s, the 'Nelsons' were regular motive power on the heaviest boat trains out of Waterloo. They continued in squadron service until their displacement by Bulleid Pacifics. In that year a number of major steam classes had been consigned for scrap and it was fortunate that the pioneer 'Lord Nelson' itself was preserved for the national collection.

In preservation 850 'Lord Nelson' has been a popular main line performer. Its more recent restoration under the auspices of the Eastleigh Locomotive Society has been extensive. Another popular main line performer since preservation is 777 'Sir Lamiel', one of the 'Arthurs'. In the custody of the 5305 Locomotive Association, it is usually based at Loughborough, on the Great Central Railway.

Nearing the end of its active career, 30850 'Lord Nelson' in British Railways livery, presents a careworn appearance at Eastleigh on 9th September 1961 (BRB/NRM).

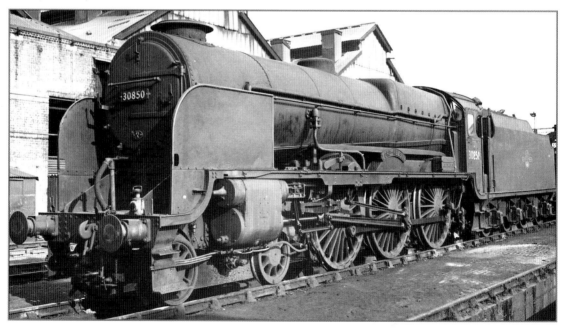

60800 'Green Arrow' pauses in York Station whilst hauling a train to Scarborough on 27th August 2000.

In the 1930s the railways were carrying increasing numbers of passengers, resulting in many trains becoming longer at a time when demands were for faster schedules. It was important that goods trains were able to keep up reasonable speeds too, thus preventing them blocking the route. Whilst big passenger locomotives were built in order to satisfy the quest for speed and strength, there was a gap in the middle range where older and underpowered locomotives struggled with the new demands.

On the LNER the answer was provided in a new design of mixed traffic (passenger and goods) locomotive, the V2 Class. It would be equally at home substituting for a Pacific on a fast express as it would hauling a train of fish vans from Grimsby to London. In fact, 4771, the first of the class, was given the name 'Green Arrow' to associate it with a new fast service of registered parcels that sped along the East Coast Route each night.

Between 1936 and 1944 there were 184 of the V2 Class built. Apart from the first 25 built at Doncaster, the rest were built at Darlington. They quickly became the staple power for many heavy passenger trains anywhere between King's Cross and Aberdeen, and the former Great Central Route from Marylebone to the East Midlands, South Yorkshire and Manchester. Arriving on the scene just before and during the Second World War, they were immediately pressed into Herculean duties. Whilst maintenance was often reduced during the war years, they proved to be robust and strong. Stories abound of their ability to move 20-coach troop trains and the like.

'Green Arrow', began its career with its allocation to Top Shed, King's Cross on 22nd June 1936. Over the next few weeks it quickly established itself as a favourite on an afternoon fast freight to Peterborough, returning with a fish train. It also was used on express passenger trains and on Christmas Eve 1936 was recorded hauling the relief 'Midday Scotsman' (a heavy load of 455 tons) at an average of 70.9mph for over 60 miles, even touching 86mph at one point.

On a railway that was blessed with an abundance of mighty Pacific power, it is easy to forget that the V2 was almost as powerful as its bigger sisters but was able to travel on routes that they could not. Many drivers preferred the V2 and certainly when well maintained they would handle beautifully. The three cylinders, when synchronised, would ensure the engine worked well…but the opposite was true if they were not! Towards the end of steam, particularly in Scotland, an 'out-of-synch' V2 made a fearsome racket and meant that the crew had a rough journey. The V2 was an easy target for diesel replacement and they succumbed quickly from 1962 to 1966 (the last was 60836 at Dundee).

The first built, 'Green Arrow', was preserved and has been a popular locomotive in recent years as it has hauled special trains across the network. Places as far apart as Carlisle, King's Cross and Plymouth have enjoyed the sight, sound and smell of a V2 as a consequence.

The icy winds were relentless. It was 14th January 1963 and crowds had braved the cold to gather at King's Cross station in London. Normally the departure of the 13.15 express to Leeds was unremarkable, but this day was different. As the bitter blast assaulted the onlookers, smoke drifted out of the tunnel at the north end of the platforms. A muffled chuffing sound preceded the appearance of a high-sided tender being propelled by a Gresley 'Pacific'. Slowly the locomotive reversed on to the waiting carriages. This was to be the last run in normal service for that legendary locomotive 'Flying Scotsman'.

As the train left King's Cross, and the crowds dispersed, many would recall a more spectacular departure from the same station, almost thirty years earlier. Again it was a winter's day, although it was murky and there was no wind. On 30th November 1934, Cecil J Allen (CJA), the doyen of train speed recorders, had been invited to King's Cross to join a trial run to Leeds. After years of apparent disinterest in speed, the railway companies were attempting to show that they were prepared to move on a notch or two. Accordingly a special run had been arranged to see how an engine not specially prepared might perform

In preservation, 'Flying Scotsman' has appeared in various guises. Here, on the turntable at Scarborough on 9th August 1987, it appears in LNER livery as 4472 with a single chimney.

if the schedules were tightened. The locomotive was 'Flying Scotsman'.

North to Leeds, the run was hardly 'normal'! For a start the train was only four coaches long. Leaving, unusually, from Platform 11 (on the suburban side of the station), CJA noted that they left in a hurry, and that a derailment on the tortuous exit from King's Cross was a distinct possibility. By the time they passed the first station, at Finsbury Park, they were roaring along at 55mph. CJA noted all the way that they were thrown about in an alarming manner, and that curves that they scarcely knew to exist suddenly made themselves felt. Arrival in Leeds was in

2 hours 31 minutes and 56 seconds – 13 minutes ahead of schedule.

Returning south, two more coaches were added to gain a different perspective on performance. Southbound the line includes what is regarded as the best stretch of racing track in Britain, the descent from Stoke Summit to Peterborough. Having reached the summit the locomotive accelerated rapidly. It was breathtaking. CJA, with his stopwatch, calculated that 98mph had been achieved over the stretch just before Essendine. However, the train included the scientifically calibrated dynamometer coach (now preserved) and the instruments showed it as having touched 100mph.

Thus, thirty years after 'City of Truro' had allegedly achieved 100mph, 'Flying Scotsman' became the first British locomotive to achieve that speed...officially.

But what are its other claims to fame? In 1924 'Flying Scotsman' had been the locomotive chosen to represent the London and North Eastern Railway at the Great British Empire Exhibition at Wembley. This was repeated in 1925 and it became etched in the minds of generations of people as the perfect example of a powerful express locomotive. On 1st May 1928, 'Flying Scotsman' was chosen to inaugurate the first of the regular non-stop runs between King's Cross and Edinburgh. This journey of 392.7 miles was made possible by the introduction of a new type of

Appearing as British Railways 60103, 'Flying Scotsman' heads out of Goodrington on the Torbay Steam Railway on 18th August 1993.

tender which could carry enough coal for the journey whilst also providing a small corridor connected to the train to enable the crew to change over without stopping. In 1928 'Flying Scotsman' gave its name (and featured) in the first sound feature film. This certainly helped to strengthen the mystique around the locomotive as the film was shown around the cinema circuits of the day.

In preservation, 'Flying Scotsman' has had an illustrious career. Saved from the scrapyard for the sum of £3000 by the incredible foresight and ingenuity of Alan Pegler, 'Flying Scotsman' has had several owners and been involved in a number of difficult financial situations. During that time, however, it has visited many parts of Britain and made new friends. It has also achieved new distinctions. On 1st May 1968 it celebrated the fortieth anniversary of its non-stop run to Edinburgh by repeating its epic journey, non-stop, albeit at slower speeds. No train of any type has done this since.

In 1969 it went to the USA and Canada, hauling an ambassadorial train for British industry. It returned to Britain in 1973. To help celebrate the bicentenary of Australia, 'Flying Scotsman' went 'down under' in 1988. It circumnavigated the globe – travelling to and from Australia in different directions. Whilst in Australia it achieved the amazing distinction of hauling the longest-distance non-stop steam train in the world, taking 9 hours and 25 minutes. This was along the 422 miles from Parkes to Broken Hill in New South Wales on 9th August 1988.

In 2004, after an uncertain period during which it was offered for sale, it was feared that this most famous of locomotives would be sold for export. Consequently a huge response from the public, combined with a matching donation from Sir Richard Branson, and a grant from the National Heritage Memorial Fund, ensured success. The 'most famous locomotive' in the world (after the fictitious 'Thomas'!) is now part of the National Collection.

Leaving the cavernous interior of York station, LNER A4 Pacific 4468 'Mallard' gets to grips with the 'Scarborough Flier' on 25th April 1987.

In the years just before the Second World War, the railways provided the quickest way between most major cities, and certainly between London and Scotland. Capturing the cream of Anglo-Scottish traffic at the expense of their rival was the aim of the two companies involved. On the East Coast Route from King's Cross, the London and North Eastern Railway (LNER) had been building up a solid reputation for speed based on its significant fleet of Pacific locomotives. But the directors needed more than that. They wanted the accolade of being the fastest. When their rivals, the London, Midland and Scottish (LMS), joined in this quest the competition hotted up.

On a Sunday morning, 3rd July 1938, a train was waiting at Barkston South Junction north of Grantham. It was a regular activity as brake testing experiments were being conducted between there and Peterborough most weekends. Sunday mornings were good opportunities as the chance of interfering with or being interfered by other trains was much reduced. The difference this morning was that, instead of the usual engine on the front, the Gresley streamlined Pacific 'Mallard' was simmering ready to go. The driver, Joe Duddington, had been the regular driver since 'Mallard' was new. He understood every inch of that locomotive.

Once the route was clear, Duddington brought the train off the branch line and it chattered off towards Peascliffe Tunnel. Track maintenance at Grantham resulted in a slow passage through the station but then the locomotive accelerated up the bank towards Stoke Tunnel. Inside the tunnel the brake technicians gradually realised that something unusual was happening. The red sparks cascading around the carriages signified that coal was hardly burned before the exhaust was carrying it out of the chimney. This engine was being pushed hard!

With York Minster on the skyline, 4468 'Mallard' races towards Haxby with a cricket festival special to Scarborough on 4th September 1986.

'Mallard' is a crowd-puller, as evidenced in this view of Beverley station when it halted whilst hauling one of the 'Mallard 88' commemorative trains on 9th July 1988.

'Mallard' was steam-tested for the first time since 1963 on 27th September 1985. It is seen here, without its streamlined casing alongside Great Northern Single No1 at the National Railway Museum, York.

Passing the summit at 85mph, it was not long before the train had reached 100miles per hour and was accelerating downhill on the long stretch to Peterborough. Faster and faster, the speed increased rapidly, soon overtaking the LMS claim of 114 mph. Faster still. Duddington recalls that it just seemed natural to travel at such a speed. When they eased off at 122mph it might all have been over but, reaching Little Bytham, Duddington squeezed that extra bit of power from the engine until 126 mph was achieved. In retrospect Duddington reckoned that they could have achieved 130mph!

The subsequent career of 'Mallard' as one of the Pacific locomotives on the East Coast Route is not particularly spectacular. Perhaps it is a reflection on the superb design and quality of the A4 Class to which it belongs that probably any one of them, in such fine fettle as 'Mallard' that day, could have equalled the record. Indeed a famous classmate 'Sir Nigel Gresley' holds the British post war steam speed record of 112 mph. But that is a long way behind the feat achieved by Joe Duddington and 'Mallard' on 3rd July 1938.

Normally 'Mallard' has pride of place in the Great Hall of the National Railway Museum in York. Behind it is the old North Eastern Railway dynamometer coach in which was recorded the fastest speed for steam...ever.

STEAMING ON

The huge size of 46229 'Duchess of Hamilton' is shown on the turntable at Scarborough where there is little room for manoeuvre. 28th August 1994.

Looking at the railway in Britain today, where a train of nine or ten coaches is considered long, it is hard to remember the time when express trains might be 50% longer. In those days frequencies were less than we are used to and so trains had to be longer. But longer means heavier, and express train schedules were often fast so inevitably the locomotives that pulled them had to combine strength with being able to accelerate and maintain high speeds. The years leading up to the Second World War saw railways across the world pushing levels of excellence ever higher.

Into such a world William Stanier was appointed by the London Midland and Scottish Railway (LMS) to design and build a fleet of locomotives. The LMS had inherited a mixed bag of locomotives when it was formed a dozen years earlier, but most were underpowered or time-expired for the new demands. Stanier was head-hunted from the Great Western and brought with him a number of practices new to the LMS. Very quickly he managed to marry the best of his upbringing with the experiences of the new environment, and new locomotives were soon rolling out of the works.

Whilst his 5MT and 8F locomotives would undoubtedly be the ones that changed the landscape, his 'Princess Coronation' Class was the pinnacle of excellence. This was designed to haul high-speed heavy trains over the Northern Fells of England and the Southern Uplands of Scotland without flinching a muscle – and it succeeded. As a matter of fashion, some of the class was streamlined.

The birth of a steam locomotive was a very special moment at any railway works. All the hours of hammering and beating on metal came together as a new locomotive was hauled out of the erecting shops in a moment as triumphant as the launch of an ocean liner. And so on 7th September 1938, the tenth of the 'Princess Coronation' class was rolled out of Crewe Works. A streamlined engine in red livery with gold stripes, this was a fashion statement in an Art Deco world. 6229 'Duchess of Hamilton' had been built for £11,302. Within two days it had entered revenue-earning service, based at Crewe North shed.

Meanwhile in the United States, proposals to celebrate the 150th Anniversary of the inauguration of George Washington as President resulted in great plans for a

Sporting an unlikely 26D shed plate (Bury), 46229 'Duchess of Hamilton' awaits departure from York on 8th June 1996.

huge exposition to be held in New York in 1939. As part of that, the LMS was invited to send a streamlined locomotive and train to tour the eastern seaboard states. The locomotive chosen was 'Duchess of Hamilton', as it was the newest of its class but, for publicity purposes, it had its identity changed with the class prototype 6220 'Coronation'.

During 1939 the locomotive and its train travelled extensively and to great acclaim. The World's Fair in New York saw the train visited by over two million people over five months but by the time the gates finally closed on 30th October the world was a very different place. Britain had been at war with Germany since 3rd September. It would have been very risky to have brought the train home and so it was stored in Baltimore. By 1941, however, the situation on Britain's railways was difficult and so plans were made to bring the locomotive home. After a difficult crossing of the Atlantic it was eventually unloaded successfully at Cardiff, returning to use on the LMS main lines on 18th March 1942. Identities were swapped back again in 1943 when both the real 'Coronation' and 'Duchess of Hamilton' (in the guise of 'Coronation') happened to be together in Crewe Works for repair.

Following the war, and the creation of British Railways in 1948, 'Duchess of Hamilton' had its streamlining removed. This was as much for ease of maintenance as anything else. It was renumbered 46229 and given smoke deflectors before taking up its traditional role on the West Coast Route of the former LMS.

After a career that saw it accumulate over one and a half million miles, it was withdrawn from service in 1963 and sold to Butlins as feature at the Minehead Holiday Camp. In 1976 it came to the National Railway Museum in York, and was steamed as a result of funding provided by its Friends organisation in 1980. Since then 46229 has been seen in many parts of the country both on preserved railways and on the main line, when not on display at York.

In 1955 there used to be a regular Saturday afternoon goods train from Gowhole Yard in Derbyshire to North Manchester. It was often used to get 'spare' locomotives back to Newton Heath shed and could provide very odd combinations. The regular 'oddity' was a venerable Midland 2F 0-6-0 in front of an almost new 9F 2-10-0. The contrast could not have been greater and it was the cause of both mirth and delight to those who saw it. The Midland locomotive was a long-chimneyed 'classic' design going back to the nineteenth century but the 9F was the brave new world's answer to an age-old problem – wagons.

From the dawn of railways until comparatively recent years, goods trains were composed of small wagons largely derived in design from the tubs that were used on the mineral tramways. Each could be hauled by a horse. With the advent of steam locomotives they were marshalled together into trains but the basic concept of the wagon remained. After the Second World War there were millions of such wagons in service on Britain's railways. Most had only individual hand-operated brakes so that they could be parked safely. Once on the move the only brakes were on the locomotive and the brake van, in which the guard rode at the rear.

92220 'Evening Star' stands impressively at Pickering on the North Yorkshire Moors Railway on 10th October 1987.

In those early post-war years it was assumed that the railways would need replacement equipment but very little thought went into new designs. However, the Standard range of locomotives, bland as it was, produced a real star. It was a goods locomotive capable of moving - and stopping – a long train of laden wagons. Known as the 9F it had ten coupled driving wheels that were small, thus producing a greater tractive effort than many other engines of the day.

The 9F was huge by British standards. Just seeing one hurling a laden coal train under a bridge, and you could see how tight the clearances were. Everything from its long boiler to the modern cab seemed to squeeze credibility.

Production of these mighty beasts was undertaken at both Crewe and Swindon and eventually ended in 1960 after 251 had been built. The last one came from Swindon. Unlike the other class members, 92220 was named – 'Evening Star'. It was a name that rekindled memories of the Great Western Railway. Painted in lined express passenger green, with copper-capped fittings, it was turned out in the best Swindon tradition. But the tide had already turned. Since 1955, railway policy had changed in favour of diesels and electrics. The network was already

Above: The powerful lines of 'Evening Star' are shown clearly as it waits to return to York with the 'Scarborough Spa Express' on 29th August 1988. This was its last time on the main line.

Below: Contrast in styles. Early Great Western is demonstrated by the reproduction 'Iron Duke' whilst the last steam locomotive built for British Railways was 'Evening Star', on the right. The pair were seen together at York on 27th September 1985.

being flooded with new modern traction. Brilliant as it was the 9F was a doomed design. It should have had a life span of 35 years but some – including 'Evening Star' – were taken out of service within five years. All had gone by 1968.

It was a terrible waste. But then times were changing too and many of the small wagons were also destined for the scrap heap. Trains with large bogie wagons, and trains carrying international containers, all at higher speeds than the 9F was designed for, took over. The landscape had changed forever.

A number of 9Fs have been preserved. In the National Railway Collection, a special place has always existed for 'Evening Star'. Its exploits on the main line since preservation have endeared it to many as a result.

STEAMING ON

As the sand drains out of the egg timer it seems to flow faster towards the end. So it seemed with the end of steam on Britain's railways. Everyone had known that the end was coming. Steam had been banished from the Western Region in 1965. It had been wiped out in Scotland in 1966; the Southern saw it go out with a bang in 1967 and the Eastern Region fizzled out by 1967. By the beginning of 1968 only the London Midland Region had viable steam and, even then, only one express locomotive: a BR Standard Class 7 Pacific, 70013 'Oliver Cromwell'.

Most of the steam action was in the Manchester and Liverpool areas going north as far as Preston and Blackpool, south into the Peak District. Gradually, like lamps going out, sheds closed to steam until by the end of July it was just Carnforth and Rose Grove (Burnley) that had an allocation. During that year it seemed that everyone wanted to savour mainline steam for the last time. Every weekend railtours using the same rundown engines criss-crossed the North West giving opportunities for a last farewell.

'Oliver Cromwell' was much in demand. It had survived for a number of reasons. Most importantly the doyen of the class, 70000 'Britannia' had been de-selected for preservation as part of the National Collection because of its poor condition upon withdrawal. In contrast

When 70013 'Oliver Cromwell' left Crewe Works on 2nd February 1967, it became the final standard gauge steam locomotive in regular service to be overhauled by British Railways. It is seen at a ceremony to mark the occasion. (NRM).

'Oliver Cromwell' had been the last steam locomotive overhauled at Crewe works – as late as 1967 - at the same time becoming the last standard gauge steam locomotive to be overhauled by British Rail. Thus, when the rest of the class suffered a mass withdrawal upon the closure of Carlisle Upperby shed at the end of 1967, 'Oliver Cromwell' was kept on to see out the end of steam.

'Oliver Cromwell' was going to haul the Duke of Edinburgh around the West Riding and Lancashire during 1967 when it was pointed out that the name had less than favourable connections with royalty and Jubilee 4-6-0 No 45562 'Alberta' was substituted at the eleventh hour.

Eventually time ran out. The last day for BR steam in ordinary service was 3rd August 1968 and Black Five 45212 performed the honours with a Preston – Blackpool South train. Next day no less than six special trains (some double headed) threaded their way across the lines of Lancashire. Then it was all over apart from 11th August and the un-named final BR commemorative train, nicknamed the 'Fifteen Guinea Special'. At a time when railtours cost a sixth of this amount it seemed as if no one would pay to be on the very last one – but they did!

Starting at Liverpool Lime Street behind Black Five 45110 the train followed Stephenson's route across Chat Moss to Manchester. From here 'Oliver Cromwell' took the train over the Settle and Carlisle route to Carlisle. Return to Manchester was behind two Black Fives, 44781 and 44871. The final trip to Liverpool was with 45110.

That final day was one of unparalleled nostalgia. It seemed as if every person with even a remote interest in railways was out to witness the occasion. As 45110 traversed George Stephenson's line there was a sense of completion, even if the occasion was sad.

But it was at Batty Moss, on remote Blea Moor, that the wildest scenes were witnessed. On the spot where the occasional lone photographer had recorded steam battling against the elements with hardly anything alive for miles around, the scene had become more akin to Blackpool on a Bank Holiday. Hundreds of photographers were poised with their cameras awaiting 'Oliver Cromwell'. Fortunately it was a glorious day and as the train came across the Ribblehead